# RHAPSODY in BLUEGRASS

## *A Christmas Jubilee*

By Joseph M. Martin • Orchestrations by Wes Ramsay

① This symbol indicates a track number on the StudioTrax CD.

*Duration: ca. 38 Minutes*


ISBN 9-781-5400-1481-8

7777 W. BLUEMOUND RD. P.O. BOX 13819 MILWAUKEE, WI 53213





Visit Hal Leonard Online at
**www.halleonard.com**

Visit Shawnee Press Online at
**www.shawneepress.com**

Contact Us:
**Hal Leonard**
7777 West Bluemound Road
Milwaukee, WI 53213
Email: info@halleonard.com

In Europe contact:
**Hal Leonard Europe Limited**
Distribution Centre, Newmarket Road
Bury St Edmunds, Suffolk, IP33 3YB
Email: info@halleonardeurope.com

In Australia contact:
**Hal Leonard Australia Pty. Ltd.**
4 Lentara Court
Cheltenham, Victoria, 3192 Australia
Email: info@halleonard.com.au

## FOREWORD

When word and music come together, there is powerful potential. Music gives wings to message and message gives purpose to song. There is no greater example of this truth than when considering the various traditions of sacred music. From lofty oratorios and noble hymns, to folk music and simple spiritual songs, the voice of faith is encouraged when shared upon the wings of song.

With the musical customs of Christmas, there is a wonderful intersection of ministry and artistry that can truly touch the heart. When we sing from this precious treasury of sacred songs, we connect with the spirit of the troubadour. We reprise our role as "storytellers," passing along our faith in tunes and texts that celebrate our faith with hopeful joy. Folk music holds a special place in the sacred lexicon, and every part of the world has its own repository of native song. This cantata is a mingling of more traditional church choral sounds with the rustic beauty of bluegrass folk music. In the joining of these two styles, I pray that something new be released into our seasonal worship gatherings. May our many voices become one song! May our differences become harmony, and may divine light decorate our hearts with the joy and grace of Christmas!

Joseph M. Martin

## PROGRAM NOTES

*RHAPSODY IN BLUEGRASS* is a celebration of pure Christmas joy. It is inspired by American folk song, bluegrass, gospel, hymn and traditional musical styles. The cantata takes the listener on the Christmas journey from prophecy to proclamation. *RHAPSODY IN BLUEGRASS* is decorated with traditional instruments and an informal narration that maintains the character of music and encourages the spirit of hope that permeates the work.

As you present the cantata, feel free to adapt your choral sound to convey the style of the work in an authentic way. Instrumentalists may feel free to improvise as they realize the score, always striving to encourage and support the singing. Soloists, likewise, should feel freedom of interpretation as they expressively deliver their musical moments.

Creative presentations may want to include a narrator who realizes the text and scripture readings with a relaxed, easygoing manner, taking on the role of a storyteller rather than a formal reader. This approach will connect with the unique musical syntax of the cantata and maintain the folk character of the work. With certain types of theatrical presentations, the choir may want to forgo traditional robes to visually represent the character of *RHAPSODY IN BLUEGRASS.*

Whatever the approach, I pray that you will find the right balance of musical and theatrical elements and bring to your community of faith a joyful moment of Christmas jubilee.

(EDITOR'S NOTE: When presenting this work with a live ensemble, you are encouraged to create moments featuring your instrumentalists. For example, in "A Little Light Was Born," have the choir sing through measure 18. Then, repeat measures 11-18 as many times as needed, allowing each player to solo individually over the chord progression. Once everyone has been featured, repeat the section one more time, allowing the players to improvise simultaneously. Following this, the song may proceed.)

# RHAPSODY IN BLUEGRASS

*A Christmas Jubilee*

**NARRATOR:**

Gather ’round, neighbors, and I’ll tell you the most glorious story ever told. It’s a story filled with miracles and wonders. A true story of how God shared His love with the world and sent His son, Jesus, to live among us. At just the perfect time, Jesus came to restore the light of hope in the hearts of the people and to announce a great season of jubilee.

Friends, this is good news for all people! There’s a new song soaring on the wind. Come, everyone, and join the music.

Listen, learn, and live!

# HEAR THE WONDROUS STORY

*Words by*
JOSEPH M. MARTIN (BMI)

*Tunes:*
**INVITATION**
*and* **BEACH SPRING**
*Arranged by*
JOSEPH M. MARTIN

* Tune: INVITATION, traditional American folk melody

9
Light born long a - go.
mf unis.
From the courts of heav-en's
9
12
Born the
glo - ry, came the Christ to earth be - low.
12
15
f
hope of ev - 'ry na - tion, born the joy of ev - 'ry
f
15
f

18
heart, Je - sus, Light of all cre - a - tion, He's the
18
21
bright and morn - ing star!
21
mf
24
2
mp unis.
Gath - er
24
f

27
friends, and join the sing - ing. Let the mu - sic soar on
mp
30
high. There are an - gels 'round us wing - ing, bring-ing
33
35
mf
glo - ry to the sky; sing - ing glo - ry in the
mp
mf

36
highest, singing glory to the Lamb. Come and
39
join with heav-en's bright - est. Christ is born in Beth-le -
42
hem.
f
dim. poco a poco

* Tune: BEACH SPRING, traditional American folk melody
Words: Charles Wesley, 1707-1788

55
56
mf
crown. Je - sus, Thou art all com - pas - sion. Pure, un -
58
unis.
bound - ed love Thou art. Vis - it us with Thy sal -
61
Tempo I (𝅗𝅥 = ca. 84)
va - tion. En - ter ev - 'ry long - ing heart.
p cresc. poco a poco

65
68
f
69
4
72
SOPRANO
mf unis.
74
ALTO
Come all peo - ple, lift your
TENOR
BASS
72
74
mf
75
voic - es. Cast a - way all doubt and fear. Clap your
mf unis.
Come all peo - ple, lift your voic - es. Cast a -
75

78
hands. Make joy - ful nois - es. Heav - en now is draw - ing
way all doubt and fear. Heav - en now is draw - ing
78
81
82
f
near. Let us all join hands to - geth - er. Come to
f
near.
81
82
f
84
heav - en's ju - bi - lee. Learn the song that lasts for -
84

89
ff
ev - er. Set your al - le - lu - ias free.
Al - le - lu - ia!

**NARRATOR:**

For many years, the old-timey prophets had told the people about the coming of the promised Savior. This great leader would teach and preach and reach out to everyone. Even the poor and the needy would be remembered. The mountains and valleys would once again ring with promise. Justice and peace would rule the earth.

Listen to these words from the Bible:
*May the King judge Your people with righteousness, and Your poor with justice. May the mountains yield prosperity for the people, and the hills ring with the music of grace.* *Psalm 72: 1-4 (adapted)*

# THE KING SHALL COME

*Words by*
JOHN BROWNLIE (1857-1925)

*Tune:* **CLEANSING FOUNTAIN**
American Folk Melody
*Arranged by*
JOSEPH M. MARTIN (BMI)

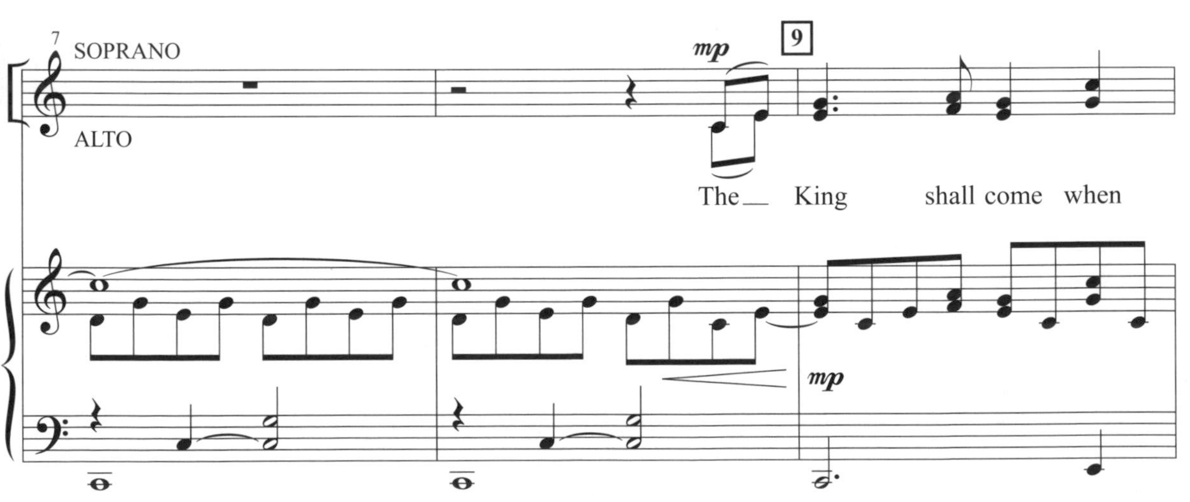

mel.
morn - ing dawns, and light tri - um - phant breaks; when
beau - ty gilds the east - ern hills, and life to joy a -
17
mf
wakes; when beau - ty gilds the east - ern hills, and
TENOR
BASS

19
life to joy a - wakes. The King shall come when
22
morn - ing dawns, and life to joy a - wakes.
25
6
dim.

27
SOLO
mp
28
O bright - er than that glo - rious morn shall
Loo loo loo loo loo loo loo
p
Loo loo loo loo
Loo loo loo loo
p
Loo loo loo loo loo loo
27
28
mp
30
this fair morn - ing be, when Christ, our King, in
loo loo loo loo loo loo loo loo loo
loo loo loo loo loo loo loo loo
loo loo loo loo loo loo loo
loo loo loo loo loo loo loo loo loo
30

33
mf
beau - ty comes, and we His face shall see.
loo loo loo
mf
f
loo and we His face shall see, when
loo loo
mf
loo loo and we His face shall see,
33
mf
36
Christ, our King, in beau - ty comes, and we His face shall
f
Christ, our King, in beau - ty comes, and we His face shall
36

39
mp
O bright - er than that glo - rious morn shall
Loo loo loo loo loo
mp
p
see.
Loo loo loo loo shall
Loo loo loo
mp
p
see.
Loo loo loo loo shall
39
mp
42
mf
7
(solo tacet to m. 62)
this fair morn - ing be.
mf
this fair morn - ing be.
mf
this fair morn - ing be.
42
cresc.
mf

44
rit.
f
45 Broader (♩= ca. 69)
The King shall come when
f
44
rit.
45 Broader (♩= ca. 69)
f
46
dim.
morn - ing dawns, and light and beau - ty brings.
dim.
46
dim.
49
rit.
mp freely
rit.
p
"O
"Hail, Christ, the Lord!" Thy peo - ple pray.
49
freely
rit.
mp
rit.
p

with sweeping expression
53
come quick - ly, King of kings."
a tempo
mf
rit.
mp
"Come quick - ly, King of kings."
p
mf
"Come quick - ly, King of kings."
53
a tempo
rit.
56
p unis.
a tempo
poco rit.
"Come quick - ly, King of
56
p
pp
p
a tempo
poco rit.
59
Gently (♩ = ca. 76)
8
kings."
59
Gently (♩ = ca. 76)

SOLO
rit.
pp
63 Slower to the end
rit.
The King shall come when morn - ing dawns.
rit.
rit.
62
63 Slower to the end
rit.
pp
rit.
66
pp
ppp
A - men.
pp
ppp
66
ppp

**NARRATOR:**

On clear cold nights, out in the country, sometimes you can see a million stars shining like silver diamonds against the dark sky. It reminds you of the greatness of God. So vast is the universe, you have to ask yourself, "Who are we that God should even consider us His children? What love would cause Him to give His very brightest star to be the light to our paths and a lamp unto our way?"

In the days before the Messiah was born, there came a star rising in the eastern sky. Just seeing its glimmer brought hope to the nation. Could the time be drawing near when God would send His Morningstar? With each passing year, they held tighter to their faith, and prayed with all their hearts for the coming of jubilee.

*I see Him, but not now; I behold Him, but not near; a star shall come forth from Jacob. A scepter shall rise from Israel.* *Numbers 24:17 (NASB)**

# STAR OF PROMISE, LIGHT OF GLORY

*Words by*
JOSEPH M. MARTIN (BMI)
*With additional words by*
CHARLES WESLEY (1707-1788)

*Tune:* **WARRENTON**
*The Sacred Harp*, 1844
*Arranged by*
BRAD NIX (ASCAP)

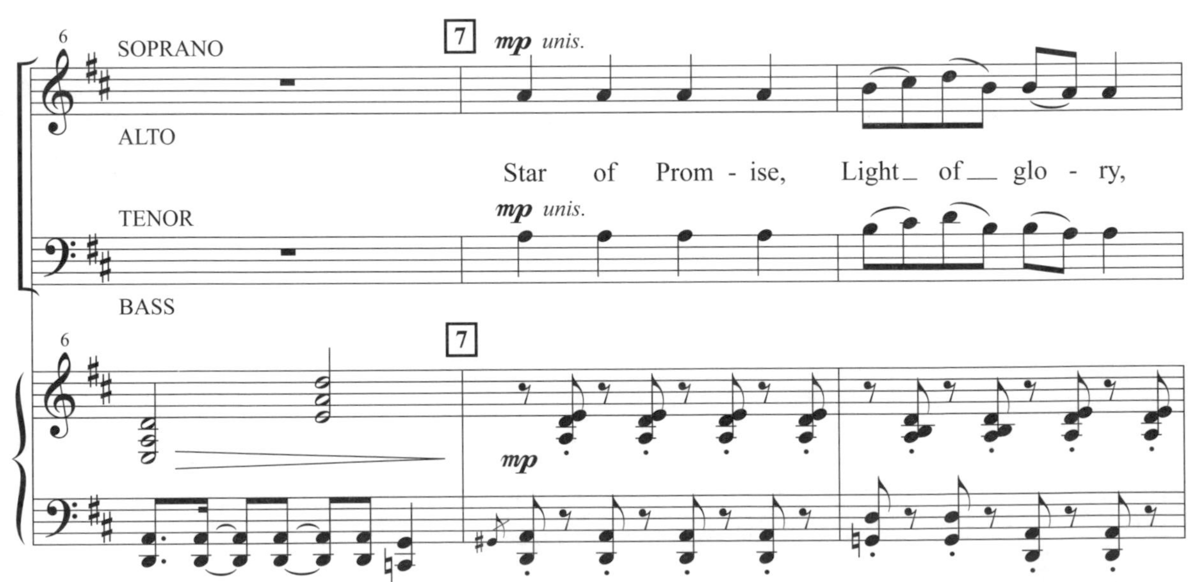

9
mf
mp unis.
come and shine_ for - ev - er-more._
Proph - ets have fore -
mf
mp unis.
9
mf
mp
12
mf
mp unis.
told_ the_ sto - ry.
Soon our long-ing eyes will see
the Lord._ There's a
mf
12
mf
mp
15
mf
great joy a-com-in'. Un-to us a Child is giv - en.
Al - le-lu - ia!_
mf unis.
15
mf

18

10

Praise the Lord!

18

21

*mp*

Star of Prom - ise, rise be - fore us. Burn a - way our

*mf* Burn a - way our

*mf* Burn a - way our

21

Burn a - way our

*mp*

*mf*

24

doubt and fear.

*mp*

Come in pow - er. Heal, re - store us.

24

*mp*

27

*mf*

Wipe a - way each

*unis.* *mp*

Wipe a - way each fall - ing tear. There's a

*mf*

Wipe a - way each

*unis.* *mp*

Wipe a - way each

27

*mf*

29

great joy a - com - in'. Un - to us a Child is giv - en.

29

*mp*

31

*mf*

Al - le - lu - ia!

Al - le - lu - ia! Praise the Lord!

*mf*

Al - le - lu - ia!

Al - le - lu - ia! Praise the Lord!

31

*mf*

* Tune: NETTLETON, Wyeth's *Repository of Sacred Music, Part Second*, 1813

50
SOPRANO
ALTO
TENOR
BASS
12
rit.
mp
Long the
rit.
53
Holding back slightly (♩ = ca. 66)
world has walked in sad - ness; yearn-ing for a bright new
mp
56
rit.
p unis.
day.
Now the
p unis.
mp
rit.

Slightly faster (♩ = ca. 88)
dawn brings sounds of glad - ness. Morn-ing breaks with
Slightly faster (♩ = ca. 88)
p
13
65
mp
gold - en ray.
Light of the
mp
65
mp
mf
world,
Light of the world,
Light of the world,
mp
mf
Light of the world,
Light of the
mf

69
rit.
f
Je - sus, Light of the world!
f
world, Je - sus, Light of the world!
69
f
rit.
mf
Tempo I (♩ = ca. 92)
73
76
14
79
S.
ff
A.
* Come, Thou long - ex - pect - ed Je - sus; born to set Thy
T.
ff
79
B.
ff

* Text: Charles Wesley, 1707-1788

82
peo - ple free. From our fears and sins re - lease us.
82
85
mf unis.
Let us find our joy in Thee. There's a
mf unis.
85
87
great joy a - com - in'. Un - to us a Child is giv - en.
87
mf

89
f
Al - le - lu - ia!
Praise the Lord of lords!
92
mf
Al - le - lu - ia!
unis.
cresc.
95
ff
Praise the Lord!

**NARRATOR:**

Now, life in those days was filled with hardships. Years of exile, slavery, and oppression took its toll on the spirit of the people. Still, there were those who kept the dream for a peaceable kingdom alive from generation to generation. They passed down the words of the prophets in songs and customs, and devotedly observed the faith. They listened to the words of the scripture and lived each day with expectation and hope.

*How beautiful on the mountains are the feet of those who bring good news, who proclaim peace, who bring good tidings, who proclaim salvation, who say to Zion, "Your God reigns!"* *Isaiah 52:7 (NIV)**

# A MORNING STAR WILL RISE

*Words and Music by*
JOSEPH M. MARTIN (BMI)

13
Star will rise. There is promise for to - mor - row,
though the night is cold and dark. Hope, come drive a -
way our sor - rows. We are look - ing for the Morn - ing Star.

21
16
21
mp
25
mf unis.
Peo - ple, search the east - ern _ sky.
mf
Soon _ a Morn-ing Star will rise.
25
mf
29
God is send - ing us _ a _ sign.
Soon a Morn - ing Star will rise.
29

33
God will fill the earth with wonder. Peace will rule in ev - 'ry heart.
37
Love will shake the world like thun - der. We are pray - ing
40
41
for the Morn-ing Star.

43
17
43
mp
48
mp
Soon a Morn - ing Star will rise.
mp unis.
Come, O come, Em - man - u - el.
48
52
Soon a Morn - ing Star will rise.
Ran - som cap - tive Is - ra - el.
52

56
unis.
Lift our long-ing eyes a-bove.
Come and fill us with Your love.
56
60
cresc. poco a poco
See the glo-rious Star is ris-ing, ris-ing, ris-ing, ris-ing with the
cresc. poco a poco
60
cresc. poco a poco
64
f
dawn.
f
64
f

68
18
70
with great celebration
f unis.
Sing and shout, the day is here.
f unis.
68
70
with great celebration
mf
f
72
unis.
Soon a Morn-ing Star will rise. Joy will wipe a-way each tear.
unis.
72
76
78
Soon a Morn-ing Star will rise. Let the earth break forth with sing-ing,
76
78

80
ev - 'ry na - tion near and far; ev - 'ry hill and val - ley ring - ing.
80
84
We are reach - ing for the Morn - ing Star!
84
87
ff
We are reach - ing for the Morn - ing Star!
ff
87
ff

**NARRATOR:**

At just the right time, God chose a young peasant girl named Mary to be the mother of the Promised One. An angel delivered the surprising news to her, and she bravely embraced her calling.

Now, Mary was promised to a devout man named Joseph. He was a humble carpenter, yet he committed to do what he could to protect Mary during those challenging days. As the time drew near for Mary to deliver her baby, they both had to travel to Bethlehem to register for the census. The road from Nazareth to Bethlehem was long and dusty, but they trusted God to guide them safely to their miracle.

The Bible records their journey in the book of Luke:
*And it came to pass in those days, that there went out a decree from Caesar Augustus that all the world should be taxed. And all went to be taxed, every one into his own city. And Joseph also went up from Galilee, out of the city of Nazareth, into Judaea, unto the city of David, which is called Bethlehem; (because he was of the house and lineage of David) to be taxed with Mary his espoused wife, being great with child.* *Luke 2:1-5 (BRG)**

# MARY WENT A-RIDING

*Words and Music by*
JOSEPH M. MARTIN (BMI)

* Tune: DETROIT, *Supplement to the Kentucky Harmony,* 1820

12
Moving ahead steadily (♩ = ca. 100)
20
(play) mp

15
SOPRANO
ALTO
TENOR
BASS
mp unis.
Sweet Ma - ry went a - rid - ing one
15

18
mp unis.
with Jo - seph, her be -
cold and frost - y night,
18

21
mf
lov - ed, and filled with ho - ly Light. To
mf
21
mf
24
Beth - le - hem they trav - eled, though she was in tra -
24
27
mp
vail. The sil - ver stars were shin - ing up -
mp
27
mp

30
32
mf
on the dust - y trail.
Lis - ten.
mf
30
32
mf
33
Lis - ten.
Hear the cold wind blow.
33
f
36
21
mf
The
36

39
road to Da - vid's cit - y was paved with man - y tears. In
mf
Oo
mf
39
mf
43
faith, they walked with cour - age, and put a - side their fears.
oo
The
43
47
faith - ful cou - ple trav - eled be - neath a win - ter
47

50
sky; and trust - ed through the shad - ows, that
50
53
mp
God would be their guide.
mp
53
mp
56
mf
Lis - ten. Lis - ten. Hear the cold wind
mf
56
mf

59
22
blow.
59
f
62
63
f unis.
And
f unis.
And then, on the ho - ri - zon, a -
62
63
65
then, on the ho - ri - zon, a - rose a bless - ed
rose a bless - ed sight. King Da - vid's town was
65

68
sight, and bathed in gold - en light! The
wait - ing, and bathed in gold - en light!
68
71
prom - ise of the jour - ney would soon be com - ing
71
74
mf unis.
true. They both would hold a Sav - ior, and
mf unis.
74
mf

77
unis.
23
He would hold them too.
unis.
77

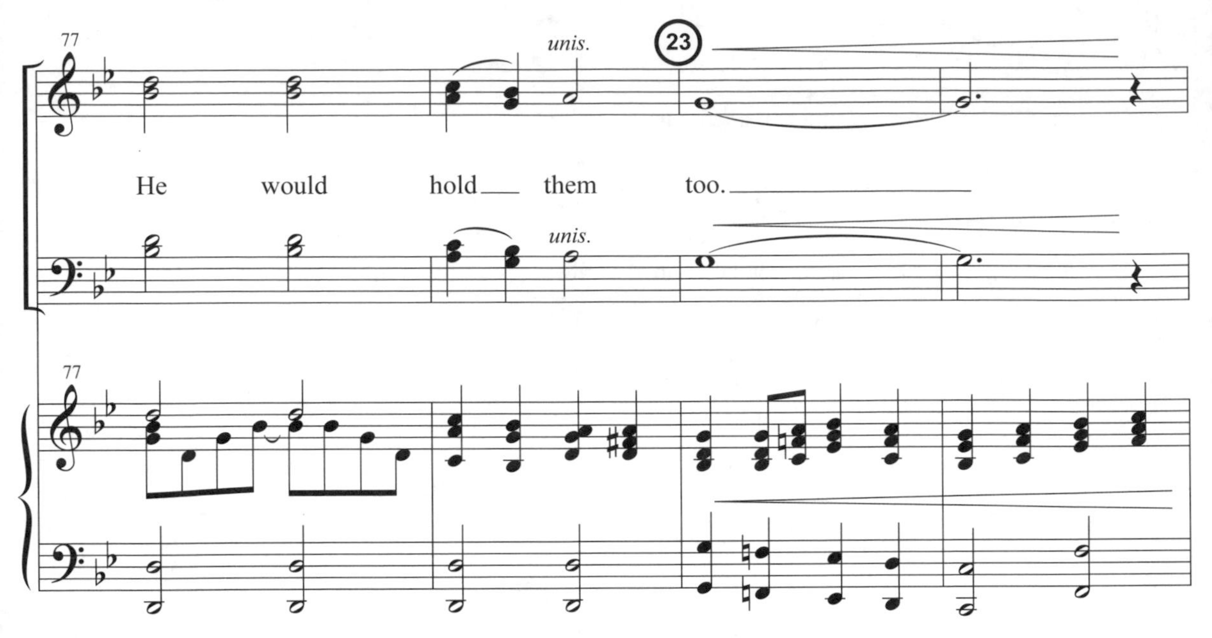

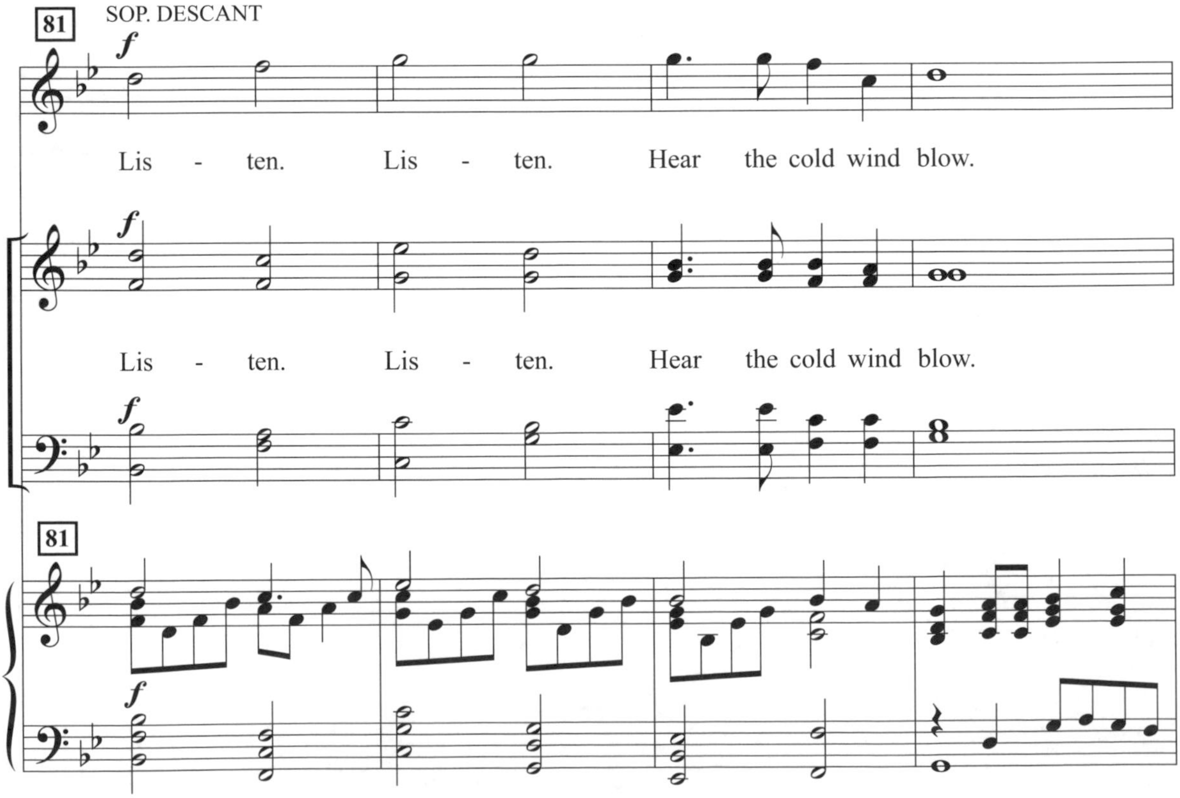

81
SOP. DESCANT
f
Lis - ten. Lis - ten. Hear the cold wind blow.
f
Lis - ten. Lis - ten. Hear the cold wind blow.
f
81
f

85
Lis - ten. Lis - ten. Hear the cold wind
Lis - ten. Lis - ten. Hear the cold wind
85
24
90
88
blow.
unis.
blow.
Hear the cold wind
unis.
mp
88
90
mp

91

mp

Hear the cold wind blow. ______ Hear the cold wind

blow.

mp

Hear the cold wind blow.

91

94

*

p

blow. ______ *Woah* ______ *woah* ______

p

Hear the cold wind blow. ______

p

Hear the cold wind

94

p

* Sing either the cued notes or the full size notes, but not both.

97

*pp* *ppp*

*woah* ___ *woah* ___

*pp* *ppp*

Hear the cold wind blow.

*pp* *ppp*

blow. ___

97

*pp* *ppp*

*rit.*

100

___

*rit.*

Hear the cold wind blow. ___

*unis.*

100

*rit.*

**NARRATOR:**

So it was in Bethlehem that Mary had her baby, just as the scriptures had promised. Joseph called His name Jesus. It wasn't in a mighty city or a golden palace that Jesus was born. She gave birth in an old barn, an old barn where animals were fed and watered. His first cradle was a manger filled with hay. Swaddling clothes and a mother's love kept Him warm that first night. The stars above were His only nightlight. God reached down and touched the earth with grace that first Christmas night and nothing has ever been the same. Yes, Bethlehem, you may be a little village, but you will always be the place where Love was born.

*...Bethlehem, though you are small among the clans of Judah, out of you will come from Me one who will be ruler over Israel, whose origins are from of old, from ancient times. Micah 5:2 (adapted)*

# O LITTLE TOWN

*Words by*
PHILLIPS BROOKS (1835-1893)

*Music by*
TOM LOUGH (ASCAP)
*Arranged by*
JOSEPH M. MARTIN (BMI)

13
14
by. Yet in thy dark streets shin - eth the ev - er - last - ing
17
Light. The hopes and fears of all the years are
21
(end solo)
met in thee to - night, are met in thee to - night.
25
Quickly, felt in two, like a folk dance (♩ = ca. 142)
mf

SOPRANO
ALTO
TENOR
BASS
26
33
mf unis.
For Christ is born of
mf unis.
Ma - ry, mild, and gath - ered all a - bove, while
mor - tals sleep, the an - gels keep their watch of won - d'ring

40
41
f
love. O morn - ing stars, to - geth - er now pro -
f
43
unis.
claim the ho - ly birth, and prais - es sing to
unis.
46
God the King, and peace to all on earth.

49
49
mf
52
27
rit.
p
How
52
mp
rit.
p
56
Slower, with expression (♩ = ca. 78)
3
si - lent - ly, how si - lent - ly, the won - drous gift is
T. only
p
Oo the won - drous gift is
56
Slower, with expression (♩ = ca. 78)
3

59
mp
giv'n! So God im - parts to hu - man hearts the
+ Basses mp
giv'n!
59
mp
62
mf
64
bless - ings of His heav'n, the bless - ings of His
mf
62
64
mf
65
rit.
Quickly again (♩ = ca. 142)
heav'n.
Quickly again (♩ = ca. 142)
65
rit.
mp

68 (28) *f unis.* 70

O___ ho - ly___ Child of

*f unis.*

O___

68 *mf* 70 *f*

71

Beth - le - hem, de - scend to___ us, we___ pray. Cast___

ho - ly___ Child, de - scend_ to___ us to - day.

71

74

out our___ sin and en - ter___ in; be___ born in us___ to -

Cast_ out our___ sin; be born_ in___ us to -

74

77 78

day. We__ hear the Christ - mas an - gels now__ the

day.

77 78

80

great glad__ tid - ings tell; *unis.* O__ come to__ us, a -

*unis.*

80

83

bide__ with__ us, our__ Lord Em - man - u - el. O__

83

86
come to us, our Lord Em -
a - bide with us,
86
89
mf
f
man - u - el, our
mf
f
89
mf
92
Lord Em - man - u - el.
92
f

**NARRATOR:**

It sure didn't take long for the news to begin spreading about the birth of Jesus. It started in an unexpected way when a group of shepherds, keeping watch over their flocks, were dazzled by a bunch of angels. There, in the open fields, the shepherds couldn't believe their eyes. "Glory to God in the highest!" the angels shouted. "Peace to people of goodwill!" These hard-working folks received a heavenly invitation to visit the miracle. So, as fast as they could go, they went to the manger and found the holy family. Jesus, the light of the world, had come! When the shepherds left, they told everyone what they had seen.

The gospel of Luke reports this way:
*And when they had seen this sight, they told everybody what had been said to them about the little child. And those who heard them were amazed at what the shepherds said. Then the shepherds went back to work, glorifying and praising God for everything that they had heard and seen.*
*Luke 2:17-18 (adapted)*

# HERE COMES THE LIGHT

*Words and Music by*
JOSEPH M. MARTIN (BMI)

* Alternate text in italics.

15
mp
Here comes the Light.
mp
mf
Dawn is break - ing. Here comes the Light. Sing to the na - tions.
15
mp
mf
18
mf
31
mp
Sing ju - bi - la - tion.
Read - y?
Are you read - y?
mp cresc.
Sing ju - bi - la - tion. Chil - dren, are you read - y?
18
mp cresc.
20
mf
21
Here comes the Light. Here comes the Light.
mf
Here comes the Light. Oh, chil - dren, here comes the Light.
20
21
mf

22
Here comes the Light. Good-bye to dark - ness, good-bye to night!
25
p cresc.
In the east - ern sky, the stars are shin - ing bright. Oh,
Down in Beth - le - hem
mf
27
glo - ry hal - le - lu - jah, chil - dren, here comes the Light!

29

Glo - ry hal - le - lu - jah, chil - dren, here

29

31 *dim. poco a poco*

Light!

*rit.*

comes the Light! Here comes the Light!

*dim. poco a poco*

comes the Light!

31

*dim. poco a poco*

*rit.*

34 32

**36 Slower, with freedom (♩ = ca. 80)**

* *p*

My Lord, what a morn - ing!

*p*

34

**36 Slower, with freedom (♩ = ca. 80)**

*p* *(Accompanist may double voices, if desired.)*

* Tune: BURLEIGH, traditional spiritual
Words: traditional spiritual, alt.

38
My Lord, what a morn-ing. Oh, my Lord, what a morn - ing, when the
42
44
bells of Christ-mas ring! My Lord, what a morn - ing.
46
when the
My Lord, what a morn-ing. My Lord, what a morn - ing,
My Lord, what a morn - ing.
33
51 Tempo I (♩ = ca. 100)
50 bells of Christ-mas ring.
bells of Christ - mas ring.
50
51 Tempo I (♩ = ca. 100)
(play)
p
mp

53
mp unis.
Here comes the Light.
mp unis.
mf
Look to heav - en!
Dawn is break - ing.
53
mf
56
mf
f
Here comes the Light.
Sing ju - bi - la - tion.
f
Sing to the na - tions.
Sing ju - bi - la - tion.
56
f
59
mf
f
Read - y?
Here comes the Light.
Are you read - y?
mf cresc.
f
Chil - dren, are you read - y?
Here comes the Light. Oh, chil - dren,
59
mf cresc.
f

61
Here comes the Light.
Here comes the Light.
here comes the Light.
61
63
Good-bye to dark - ness, good - bye to night!
63
65
mp
cresc.
In the east - ern sky, the stars are shin - ing bright.
Oh,
Down in Beth - le - hem
mp
cresc.
f
f
65
mp
cresc.
f

67 (34)

glo - ry hal - le - lu - jah, chil - dren, here comes the Light!

67

69

Light!

Light!

*sfz* *sfz*

*sfz* Light!

Light! *sfz*

*sfz* Light! *p* Oh, chil - dren,

69

71

*p*

Here comes the Light. Here comes the Light. Good-bye to dark - ness,

*p*

here comes the Light.

71

*p*

74
cresc. poco a poco
good-bye to night! In the east - ern sky, the stars are
Down in Beth - le - hem
cresc. poco a poco
74
cresc. poco a poco
76
shin - ing bright. Oh, glo - ry hal - le - lu - jah, chil - dren,
76
78
f
79
here comes the Light! Oh, glo - ry hal - le - lu - jah, chil - dren.
f
78
79
f

DESCANT (a few sopranos)
80
f
rit.
Hal - le - lu - jah! Here comes the
rit.
Hal - le - lu - jah! Here comes the
80
rit.
Slower 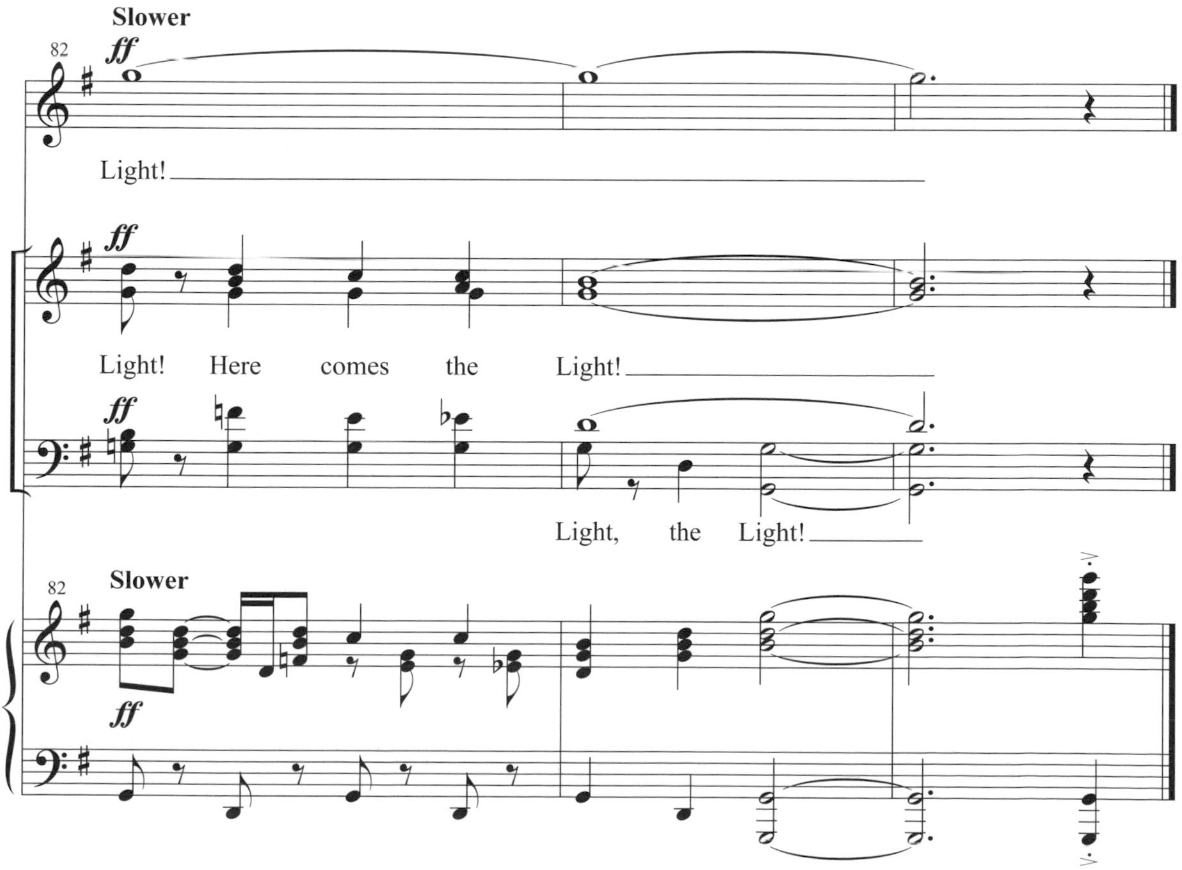
82
ff
Light!
ff
Light! Here comes the Light!
ff
Light, the Light!
82
Slower
ff

**NARRATOR:**

A new light was shining in the darkness! A great star of promise was rising over the land! A new day of hope was dawning for all the people. Even wise men from far away were befuddled by the meaning of the bright, new star they had seen in the sky. Well, they were desperate for answers, and they assembled a big caravan and headed off across the desert on a great quest. Following the star, they arrived at last in Bethlehem.

Now, listen to the gospel of Matthew:
*And now the star, which they had seen in the east, went in front of them as they travelled until at last it shone immediately above the place where the little child lay.* *Matthew 2:9-10 (PHILLIPS)**

# A CHRISTMAS ANSWER

*Words by*
WILLIAM C. DIX (1837-1898), alt.

*Music by*
JOSEPH M. MARTIN (BMI)
*Incorporating Tune:*
**O WALY, WALY**
Traditional English Melody

35 **Slowly, freely** (♩ = ca. 76)

ACCOMP.

*p*

4 *rit.* **Flowing** (♩ = ca. 108) *mp*

16
3
— is sleep - ing; whom an - gels
3
19
greet ___ with an - thems _ sweet,
22
and _ while the shep - herds, their watch are
25
36
keep - ing? ___

SOPRANO SOLO
29
mp
What Child is this,
ALTO SOLO
mp
What Child is this, up - on the
SOPRANO
29
mp
ALTO
Oo
mp
TENOR
BASS
29
31
up - on the straw, gen - tle
straw where gen - tle lambs
31
oo
31

34
lambs are feed - ing;
are feed - ing; the prom - ised
34
oo
34
37
the prom - ised Son, the Ho - ly
Son, the Ho - ly One?
37
37

37
One?
Is this the One re -
Is this the Sav - ior, our world re -
deem - ing, re - deem - ing?
deem - ing, re - deem - ing? This, this is
45
The world re - deem - ing? This, this is

46
f
Je - sus Christ the King,
whom shep - herds
Je - sus Christ the King,
Je - sus Christ the King,
whom shep - herds
49
guard
and an - gels sing.
rit.
whom shep - herds guard and an - gels sing.
guard
and an - gels sing.
3

52
ff
53 a tempo
Come now and wor - ship, wor - ship Him with
ff
Come now and wor - ship Him with
52
53 a tempo
ff
Come and wor - ship Him with
ff
52
53
a tempo
ff
55
song, with praise and laud, the
f
song, with praise and laud, the
55
f
song, with praise and laud, the
f
55
f

* Words: Isaac Watts, 1674-1748

67
come.
Let earth re - ceive
the Lord is come.
Let earth re -
70
her glo - ri - ous King.
Let ev - 'ry
mf
ceive her glo - ri - ous King.
73
f
heart
pre - pare Him room,

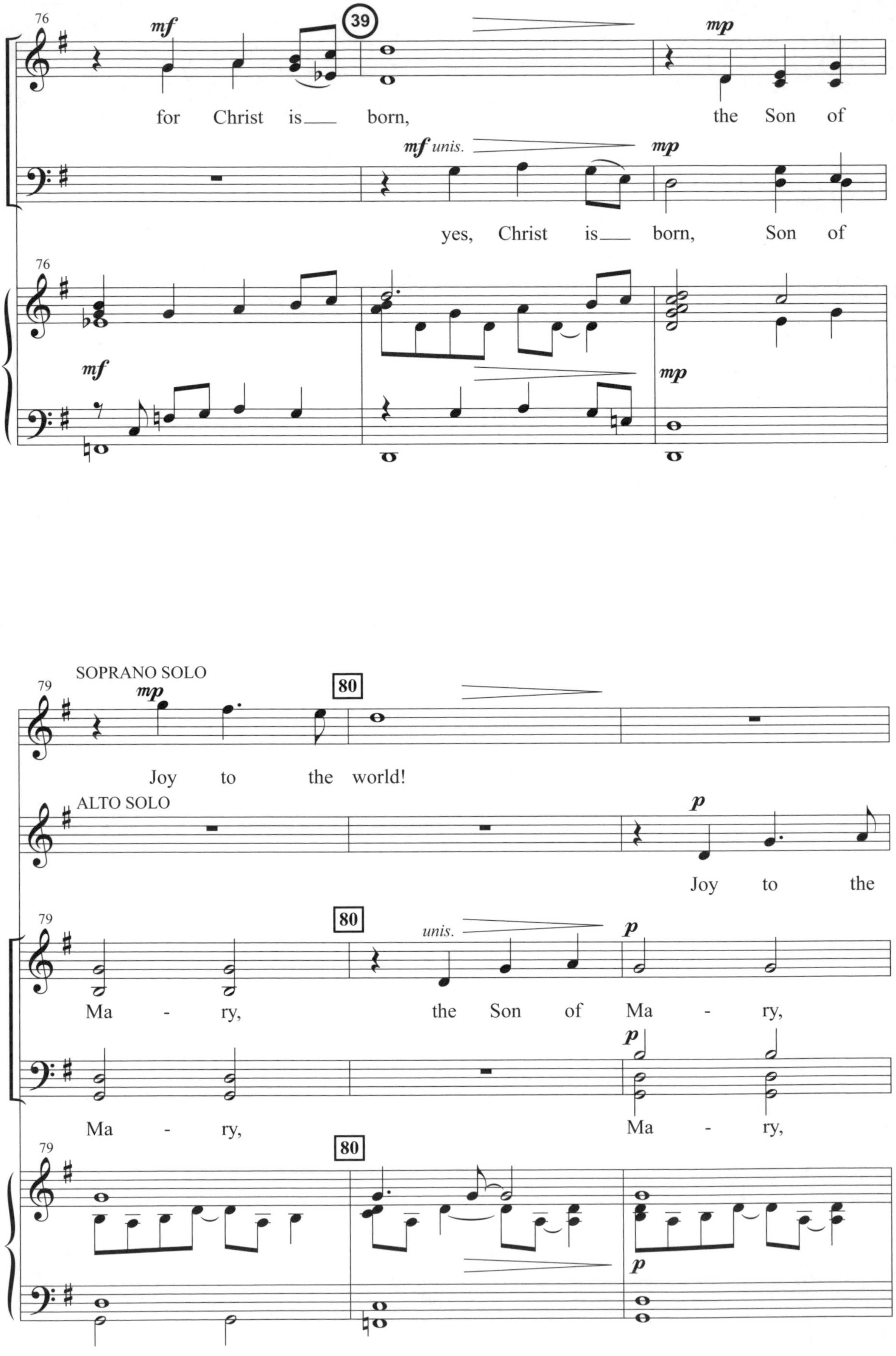

79
SOPRANO SOLO
mp
80
Joy to the world!

ALTO SOLO
p
Joy to the

79
80
unis.
p
Ma - ry, the Son of Ma - ry,

p
Ma - ry, Ma - ry,

79
80
p

82
pp
Joy to the world!
world!
the Son of Ma - ry, the Son of
Ma - ry, Ma - ry, Ma - ry.
85
rit.
Slowly
The Son of Ma - ry.
Joy to the world!
Ma - ry.
Oo

**NARRATOR:**

This, then, was the story of how Jesus, the Christ, was born. Of course, it was only the beginning of how Jesus changed the world with His most extraordinary life. That little light that was first seen in a cattle stall in Bethlehem would soon flood the whole world with new hope. That glorious light still shines today, and the darkness of this old world has never overcome it. Because of the gift of Jesus, we are now His children of light. Like the moon on a cloudless night, we can reflect the rays of His goodness for all to see. Working together, washed in His glory, filled with His spirit, we are His children of light!

*Arise, shine; for your light has come, and the glory of the LORD is now risen upon you. Isaiah 60:1 (adapted)*

# A LITTLE LIGHT WAS BORN

*Words and Music by*
JOSEPH M. MARTIN (BMI)

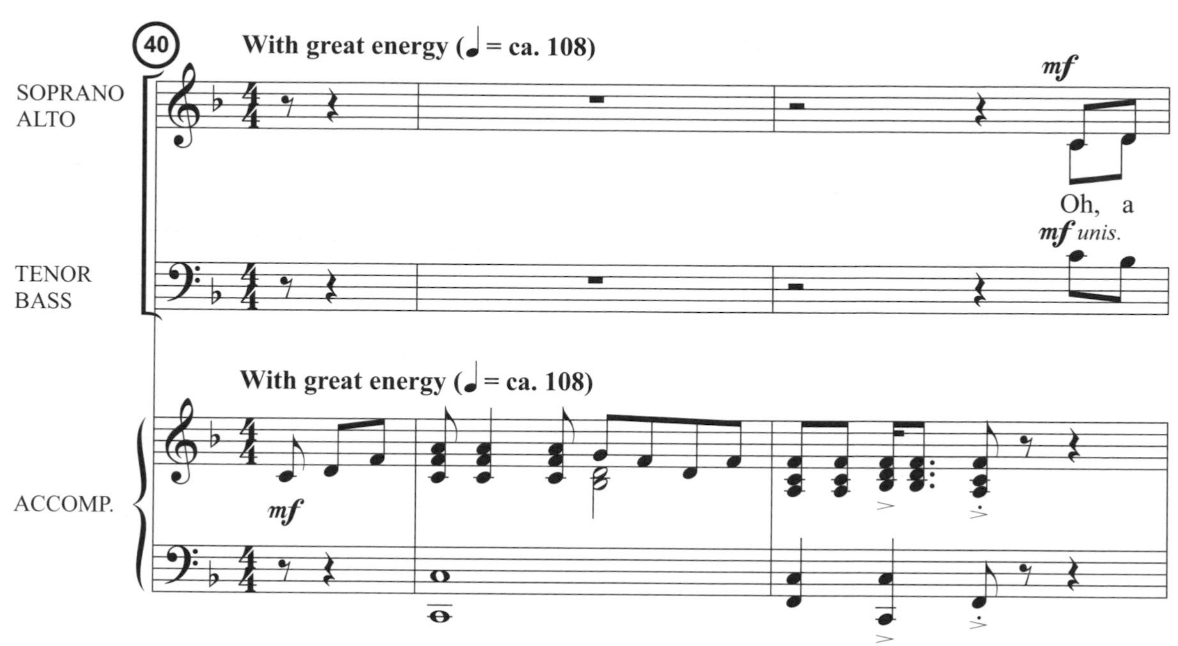

* "li'l" pronounced "liddle."

6
Beth - le-hem. Oh, a li'l Light was born down in Beth - le - hem. Oh,
6
9
41
mp unis.
Je - sus is the Light of the world. Oh, a
unis.
9
11
li'l song was born in the hush of night. Oh, a
p lightly
Lit - tle song was born in the hush of the night. A
11
mp

13
li'l song was born in the hush of night. Oh, a
lit - tle song was born in the hush of the night. A
13
15
li'l song was born in the hush of night; oh,
lit - tle song was born in the hush of night; oh,
15
17
mf
42
molto rit.
Je - sus is the Light of the world.
mf
Je - sus is the Light of the world.
17
mf
molto rit.

Slower, freely, with a swing (♩ = ca. 88)
20
SOLO
mf
In - to our dark - ness,
mf
Oh, a li'l Light was born. Oh, a
mf unis.
20
Slower, freely, with a swing (♩ = ca. 88)
23
Oh, in - to our emp - ty hearts,
li'l Light was born.
Oh, a
23

26

28

in - to our

lit - tle love was born;

26

28

29

43

allarg.

(end solo)

si - lence,

allarg.

*unis.*

came a song of peace and joy.

Oh, a

came a song of peace, of peace and joy.

29

allarg.

32
Tempo I (♩ = ca. 108)
cresc. poco a poco
li'l Light was born, li'l Light was born,
unis. cresc. poco a poco
Li'l Light was born. Li'l Light was
32
Tempo I (♩ = ca. 108)
cresc. poco a poco
34
li'l Light was born in Beth - le - hem.
Oh, a
born in Beth - le - hem.
34
37
li'l Light was born in Beth - le - hem.
Oh, a
unis.
37
Gliss.

39
li'l Light was born down in Beth - le - hem. Oh, a
39
41
li'l Light was born down in Beth - le - hem. Oh, a li'l Light was born down in
41
44
44
Beth - le - hem. Oh, Je - sus is the Light of the
44

46 DESCANT

*f* *with great rejoicing*

Al - le - lu - ia! Oh, a lit - tle Light was

*with great rejoicing*
*unis.*

world. Oh, a li'l Light was born down in

*with great rejoicing*
*unis.*

Lit - tle Light was born down in

46

*with great rejoicing*

48

born in Beth - le - hem; lit - tle Light was

Beth - le - hem. Oh, a li'l Light was born down in

Beth - le - hem. Oh, a lit - tle Light was born down in

48

50

born in Beth - le - hem; li'l Light was born down in

Beth - le - hem. Oh, a li'l Light was born down in

Beth - le - hem. A lit - tle Light was born down in

50

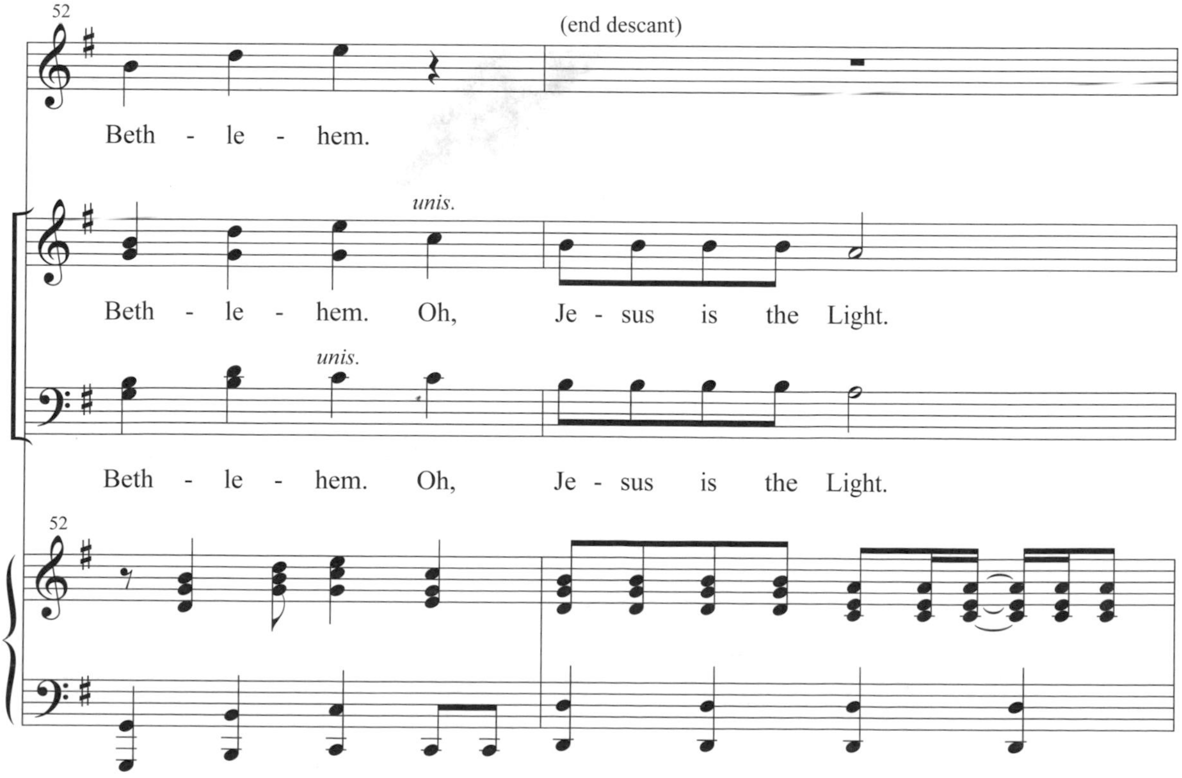

52

(end descant)

Beth - le - hem.

*unis.*

Beth - le - hem. Oh, Je - sus is the Light.

*unis.*

Beth - le - hem. Oh, Je - sus is the Light.

52

54
55
Je - sus is the Light. Oh, Je - sus is the
56
rit. al fine
ff
Light of the world; Light of the
59
world!
Gliss.